The Japanese Garden

Islands of Serenity

Photographs by HARUZO OHASHI

Each photo caption is described as follows:
Katsura Rikyu Stepping Stones Momoyama Era Kyoto
Title   Item   Time   Place

Published by Graphic-sha Publishing Co., Ltd.
1-9-12 Kudankita, Chiyoda-ku, Tokyo, 102-0073 Japan.

Distributors:
United States:Kodansha America, Inc., through Oxford University Press,
  198 Madison Avenue, New York, NY 10016.
Canada:Fitzhenry & Whiteside Ltd., 195 Allstate Parkway, Markham,
  Ontario L3R 4T8.
United Kingdom and Europe:Premier Book Marketing Ltd., Clarendon House,
  52, Cornmarket street, Oxford OXI 3HJ.
Australia and New Zealand:Bookwise International, 54 Crittenden Road,
  Findon, South Australia 5023.
Asia and Japan:Japan Publications Trading Co., Ltd., 1-2-1,
  Sarugaku-cho, Chiyoda-ku, Tokyo, 101-0064 Japan.

First Printing:April 1997
Second Printing:August 2000

ISBN0-87040-989-1

Printed in Japan

The Japanese Garden

Islands of Serenity

Contents

JAPANESE GARDEN (A BRIEF IMPRESSION)

SIMPEI KUSANO (Poet)

I am presently living at Tenzan Bunko in the sparsely populated village of Kawauchi located in the mountain range of Abukuma, and recuperating after my discharge from the hopsital. I sat and wrote this poem, "A Garden Is Never Finished," at this same desk that I have sat in day after day in the same room gazing at the same garden. Even now I feel the emotions it evokes stirring in me. This is the poem.

> A garden of only large rocks and small stones may be fine.
> A garden of merely pebbles alone may be fine.
> A garden of no water flowing may be fine.
> However, with trees, shrubs, and ferns
> A garden is never finished.
>
> A tree grows, withers and dies.
> A shrub grows, withers and dies.
> And moss grows.
> As water changes with the whims of heaven,
> The garden becomes famished.
>
> The drama of the heavens pervades.
> It may caress or lay rage.
> The ivy plant like a living creature
> Moves unseen by all except by nature.
> Its contour is demolished.
>
> This is the fate of the garden.
> My life dies and relives with the fate of the garden.
> Wishing to live such a way.

This feeling will stay forever with me.

At Tenzan Bunko, Katsumi Yamamoto designed the thatched roof bunko (library), while I designed the garden. It has been 20 years since I first started on the garden. It is located at the breast of the mountain but I did not use a single yen in its construction. Not a tree or shrub was brought from the nursery. The gigantic rocks brought in by cranes and trucks, in addition to the tremendous amount of labor, were all free of cost. Within the range of the mountains in my village no public or private expenses were entailed and no matter how many trees or rocks I had them transport not a grievance was voiced. In the beginning the garden, which was carved out in the middle of the mountain by bulldozer, did not have a single tree or blade of grass. Lacking plans on what kind of garden I wanted, I dug up some large withered maple and chestnut trees after some consideration and planted the three trees. This began the construction of my garden. I then wrote the poem, "A Garden Is Never Finished."

Of the ninety-six photographs in this book by Haruzo Ohashi, forty-six were taken of Kyoto gardens. The locations of the others range from Aomori to Kagoshima and Okinawa, running vertically through the Japanese archipelago.

I had no idea of Ohashi's secret love of gardens over the many years of our acquaintance. I don't know what plans he had when he first set out to photograph gardens, however I do know that no one else has such a strong devotion to them or invests such energy in portraying them.

(There were Tauto and Hurn, however, I wonder how much westerners know of Japanese gardens. This collection is one chance to acquaint others with the beauty of Japan.)

In my poem when I wrote that "A garden of merely pebbles alone may be fine," I was alluding in part to the rock garden at the Ryoan-ji Temple. Unlike trees and plants, rocks are immobile, although the beautiful lines and ripples can be demolished by one night of heavy rain. The term "may be fine" is not absolute. It becomes "unfinished" by the unexpected downpour. To prevent it from being "unfinished" the garden must be repaired and put back to its original form.

The moss garden at the Saiho-ji Temple is nice; however, if there are weeds growing among the moss, it is marred. I do not scorn weeds. As a matter of fact, there are some instances where they are necessary for the garden. The question of propriety is decided by the dialogue between man and weed. Also whether moss adheres to rocks is determined by natural consequences. Garden plants are plants, but at the same time they are living creatures, as evidenced by their trembling. When I was healthy I always came up here once a year and each time the garden's features underwent a transformation. To me a garden is forever unfinished. Perhaps its grand original form should be constant. Growing a garden is everyone's dream and this dream produces the original form of the garden. I believe it is as stated in the poem.

Induced by Ohashi, I became distracted. No, I was distracted in the beginning, but above all, I was enticed by the pictures. The enticement was refreshing. I truly want to repeat here again that (there were Tauto and Hurn.....)

Editorial Director: Kakuzo Akahira

Design: Hiroto Kumagai

1 *Katsura Rikyu Stepping Stones Momoyama Era Kyoto*

2 *Katsura Rikyu The Front Garden of the Study Room Momoyama Era Kyoto*

3 *Kyoto Imperial Palace Osuzumi-sho Maenakajima Edo Era Kyoto*

4 *Shugaku-in Rikyu Kami no Chaya Edo Era Kyoto*

5 *Shugaku-in Rikyu Nishihama at Sunset Edo Era Kyoto*

7 *Daisen-in Karetaki Stone Grouping Muromachi Era Kyoto*

8 *Daitoku-ji Karetaki Stone Grouping Edo Era Kyoto*

9 *Sokoku-ji Karesansui Edo Era Kyoto*

10 *Ryozoku-in Karesansui Edo Era Kyoto*

11 *Ginkaku-ji Ginsanada Muromachi Era Kyoto*

12 *Ryoan-ji Karesansui Muromachi Era Kyoto*

13 *Saiho-ji Moss Garden Kamakura Era Kyoto*

14 *Saiho-ji Around the Island Kamakura Era Kyoto*

15 *Sento Imperial Palace The Central Part of Chitei Edo Era Kyoto*

16 *Tenryu-ji Taki Stone Grouping Kamakura Era Kyoto*

17 *Joruri-ji A Complete View Heian Era Kyoto*

18 *Kinkaku-ji A Complete View Kamakura Era Kyoto*

19 *Kinkaku-ji Taki Stone Grouping Kamakura Era Kyoto*

20 *Sanpo-in Sanzon Stone Grouping Momoyama Era Kyoto*

21 *Nijo-jo Gogan Stone Grouping Momoyama Era Kyoto*

23 *Katsura Rikyu Misaki-gata Lantern Momoyama Era Kyoto*

22 *Chijaku-in Taki Stone Grouping Edo Era Kyoto*

24 *Shinnyo-in Urizane-gata Lantern Momoyama Era Kyoto*

25 *Joju-in A Complete View Edo Era Kyoto*

26 *Honpo-ji Karetaki Stone Grouping Momoyama Era Kyoto*

28 *Manshu-in Ishibashi Stone Grouping Edo Era Kyoto*

29 *Nishi Hongan-ji Kame Stone Grouping Edo Era Kyoto*

30 *Konchi-in Tsuru Stone Grouping Edo Era Kyoto*

31 *Ikkyu-ji Karesansui at the East Garden Edo Era Kyoto*

33 *Nanzen-ji A Complete View Edo Era Kyoto*

34 *Tokai-an A Complete View of the Courtyard Edo Era Kyoto*

35 *Omote Senke Around the Zangetsu-tei Momoyama Era Kyoto*

36 *Ura Senke At the Yuin Edo Era Kyoto*

37 *Mushanokoji Senke At the Middle Gate Edo Era Kyoto*

38 *Yabunouchi Soke Around the Machiai Edo Era Kyoto*

39 *Koho-an Sanunjo Tsukubai Edo Era Kyoto*

40 *Omote Senke Fushin-an Tsukubai Momoyama Era Kyoto*

41 *Mushanokoji Senke Kankyu-an Tsukubai Edo Era Kyoto*

42 *Shojuraigo-ji A Water Basin Momoyama Era Shiga*

43 *Tokai-an Ichimonji Water Basin Edo Era Kyoto*

44 *Katsura Rikyu Katsura-gaki Momoyama Era Kyoto*

45 *Kinkaku-ji Kinkakuji-gaki Kamakura Era Kyoto*

46 *Koho-an Yarai-gaki Edo Era Kyoto*

47 *Yabunouchi Soke Teppo-gaki Edo Era Kyoto*

48 *Mr. Seido's Seibi-en Garden Taki Stone Grouping Meiji Era Aomori*

49 *Motsu-ji Nakajima Stone Grouping Heian Era Iwate*

50 *Yosan-ji Ookarikomi at the Central Part Momoyama Era Akita*

51 *Gyokusen-ji A Complete View Edo Era Yamagata*

52 *Rinno-ji The Central Island Edo Era Tochigi*

53 *Nonin-ji Taki Stone Grouping Edo Era Saitama*

54 *Kencho-ji A Complete View Edo Era Kanagawa*

55 *Kyu Shiba Rikyu The Central Part of Chitei Edo Era Tokyo*

56 *Choraku-ji Chitei and Tsukiyama Edo Era Shizuoka*

57 *Manko-ji Sanzon Stone Grouping Edo Era Aichi*

58 *Erin-ji Taki Stone Grouping Kamakura Era Yamanashi*

59 *Daizen-ji Tsukiyama Shudan Stone Grouping Edo Era Yamanashi*

60 *Jizo-ji A Complete View Edo Era Nagano*

61 *Eihou-ji Bonnongan Falls Kamakura Era Gifu*

62 *Kenroku-en Kotoji-gata Lantern Edo Era Ishikawa*

63 *Rinno-ji Multi-story Stone Tower Edo Era Tochigi*

64 *Rakuraku-en Daikaku-gata Lantern Era Unspecified Shiga*

65 *Koraku-en Hotaru-gata Lantern Edo Era Okayama*

66 *Kenroku-en Seisonkaku Tea Garden Edo Era Ishikawa*

67 *Seisui-en Taki Stone Grouping Edo Era Niigata*

68 *The Site of Mr. Asakura's Residence Suwakan Ato Stone Grouping Momoyama Era Fukui*

69 *Kenroku-en The Island of Chitei Edo Era Ishikawa*

70 *Saimyo-ji A Complete View Edo Era Shiga*

71 *Daichi-ji A Complete View Edo Era Shiga*

72 *Kitabatake-jinja Gogan Stone Grouping Muromachi Era Mie*

73 *Enman-in A Complete View Edo Era Shiga*

74 *Fumon-in Karetaki Stone Grouping Edo Era Wakayama*

75 *Negoro-ji Taki Stone Grouping Edo Era Wakayama*

76 *Tentoku-in Karetaki Stone Grouping Momoyama Era Wakayama*

77 *Hokke-ji A Complete View Edo Era Nara*

78 *Gangyo-ji A Complete View Momoyama Era Nara*

79 *Raikyu-ji Tsurushima and Ookarikomi Momoyama Era Okayama*

80 *Koraku-en The Central Part of the Chitei Edo Era Okayama*

81 *Mr. Fukada's Private Garden Stone Bridge and Sanzon Stone Grouping* *Kamakura Era Tottori*

82 *Shukkei-en The Island and the Stone Bridge Momoyama Era Hiroshima*

83 *Iko-ji Kameshima Muromachi Era Shimane*

84 *Mr. Ogawa's Private Garden A Complete View Muromachi Era Shimane*

85 *Mr. Katsura's Private Garden A Complete View Edo Era Yamaguchi*

86 *Ritsurin-en The Island Edo Era Kagawa*

87 *Ritsurin-en A Complete View Edo Era Kagawa*

88 *Kenroku-en Gangyo Stone Bridge Edo Era Ishikawa*   89 *Koraku-en Yatsuhashi Edo Era Okayama*

90 *Tamon-ji Taki Stone Grouping Kamakura Era Tokushima*

91 *Gansho-ji A Complete View Kamakura Era Tokushima*

92 *Hokoku-ji A Complete View Muromachi Era Ehime*

93 *Sennyo-ji Around the Island Edo Era Fukuoka*

94 *Mr. Mori's Private Garden Taki Stone Grouping Edo Era Kagoshima*

95 *Suizen-ji A Complete View Edo Era Kumamoto*

96 *Mr. Ishigaki's Private Garden A Complete View Edo Era Okinawa*

1 Katsura Rikyu, "Stepping Stones", Momoyama Era (Kyoto)
The Katsura Rikyu, arranged as a stroll garden, displays ideal beauty no matter which portion of it is seen. To guide us, the garden is strewn with stepping stones of varied designs. The feel of rock and moss which are well matched with each other can be considered an essential element of the Japanese garden.
SINAR P NIKKOR 210mm F5.6 f22 1/15 EPR

2 Katsura Rikyu, "The Front Garden of the Study Room", Momoyama Era (Kyoto)
In a sense the front garden of the study room is the face of Katsura Rikyu. It was built by Prince Tomohito of Hachijo and Prince Tomotada. Even though the building is two generations old, its architectural beauty is still fresh and modern, the result of the elaborate care taken with its design.
SINAR P NIKKOR 90mm F4.5 f22 1/15 EPR

3 Kyoto Imperial Palace, "Osuzumi-sho maenaka-jima", Edo Era (Kyoto)
The water garden is about 7,000 m² (seventy thousand square feet) wide. The pond near Osuzumisho in the inner garden was designed with emphasis on the stream, accentuated with the three islands situated in it. The stepping stones, stone bridge and stone groupings for shore protection compose a landscape full of variety. Together with the flowers of each season, they bring about a world of elegance.
SINAR P FUJINON 210mm F5.6 f22 1/15 EPR

4 Shugaku-in Rikyu, "Kami no Chaya", Edo Era (Kyoto)
The beauty of the Shugaku-in garden lies in its great harmony with nature: The spring with its cherry blossoms, the fall blazing with red leaves and the winter with its fluttering snow flakes. Those who visit here, whatever the season, will never be disappointed.
LINHOF KARDAN NIKKOR 90mm F4.5 f22 1/15 EPR

5 Shugaku-in Rikyu, "Nishihama at Sunset", Edo Era (Kyoto)
There is no other Japanese garden that incorporates nature as this one does. Nishihama at dusk viewed from the Momijidani area of Kami no Chaya is so dynamic that man-made elements in it are hardly noticeable.
LINHOF KARDAN NIKKOR 90mm F4.5 f16 1/2 EPR

6 Shugaku-in Rikyu, "The Snowy Kami no Chaya", Edo Era (Kyoto)
Shugaku-in under snow displays even more clearly the sublime integrity of natural beauty and artificial beauty. Photographing it during a heavy snowfall was hard but I was moved to do so by the ex-Emperor Gomizuno's majestic planning and superb idea of chosing this site and designing this garden.
LINHOF KARDAN NIKKOR 90mm F4.5 f8 1/60 EPR

7 Daisen-in, "Karetaki Stone Grouping", Muromachi Era (Kyoto)
The garden is typical of dry landscapes. Steep mountains and deep valleys are expressed in a brief space of only a little more than 100 m² (one thousand square feet). The thin line of water streaming out of the depths of the mountain becomes a wide river and flows into the vast ocean. The concept of water, symbolized by white sand, is peculiar to the Japanese garden.
LINHOF KARDAN SYMMAR 150mm F5.6 f22 1/4 EPR

8 Daitoku-ji, "Karetaki Stone Grouping", Edo Era (Kyoto)
Although there are numerous ways of symbolic expression by means of great stones, this dry waterfall expressed with three stones is a magnificent composition. The technique was frequently used in the early Edo period. Teishi set at the center represents a watershed stone.
LINHOF KARDAN FUJINON 210mm F5.6 f22 1/4 EPR

9 Sokoku-ji, "Karesansui", Edo Era (Kyoto)
This is a simple, flat-type dry graden suitable for a Zen temple. As a whole, the expression is clear and magnanimous. The stone grouping in the east was partially redone in the Showa Era. The artificial hill built in the background and the flat space create a double structure effect.
SINAR P SUPERANGULON 75mm F8 f8 1/15 EPR

10 Ryozoku-in, "Karesansui", Edo Era (Kyoto)
Besides streams, large rivers and oceans, the white sand represents such abstract patterns as ripples, swirls or checks. The sand scrolls in this photograph enable the limited space to appear wider and stress the cleanliness.
SINAR P SYMMAR 150mm F5.6 f22 1/15 EPR

11 Ginkaku-ji, "Ginsanada", Muromachi Era (Kyoto)
Yoshimasa Ashikaga had a passion for gardens. One of the features of this garden, a design based on his idea, is Ginsanada (silvery sand sea). When the moon rises above Tsukimachi-yama on the east side, the sand spread here ripples with a silvery glint and the Land of Happiness presents itself.
SINAR P NIKKOR 90mm F5.6 f22 1/15 EPR

12 Ryoan-ji, "Karesansui", Muromachi Era (Kyoto)
Fifteen stones are scattered in white sand. One may take them as islands on the sea or a hazardous path. This is an adaptable space that has numberless interpretations according to each viewer's mind. It may be called the garden to make viewers philosophize.
LINHOF KARDAN SUPERANGULON 75mm F8 f22 1/8 EPR

13 Saiho-ji, "Moss Garden", Kamakura Era (Kyoto)
Stones, water and mosses are important elements in composing gardens. Particularly famous are the mosses of Saiho-ji. When touched by hand, they feel like an infant's skin. Their vivid green in the rainy season is really unforgettable.
LINHOF KARDAN SYMMAR 150mm F5.6 f22 1/8 EPR

14 Saiho-ji, "Around the Island", Kamakura Era (Kyoto)
The garden existed before Muso Kokushi came to live in this temple but its name was changed from Saiho Jodo-ji to Saiho-ji in 1339 when this famous priest and garden designer arrived here. The unearthly atmosphere that fills the entire area stimulates our aspiration for a Pure World away from the secular society.
SINAR P NIKKOR 90mm F4.5 f32 1/2 EPR

15 Sento Imperial Palace, "The Central Part of Chitei", Edo Era (Kyoto)
Like Shugaku-in, this grand water garden is closely related to the ex-Emperor Gomizunoo. The building was started in 1569 under the leadership of Enshu Kobori. The south pond has a sandy beach covered with cobblestones. The exquisitely curved shoreline is even more attractive with varied tints of flowers from season to season.
SINAR P NIKKOR 90mm F4.5 f22 1/15 EPR

16 Tenryu-ji, "Taki Stone Grouping", Kamakura Era (Kyoto)
The area around the waterfall stone grouping in the depths of the garden was designed by Doryu Rankei. The stone bridge, the waterfall stone grouping, Rigyo-seki, Enzan-seki. none of them fails to surprise us because of his distinguished ability with artistic formations. This stone grouping, which expresses great forcefulness, demonstrates the highest standard of the Japanese garden-making technique.
SINAR P FUJINON 210mm F5.6 f22 1/2 EPR

17 Joruri-ji, "A Complete View", Heian Era (Kyoto)
The temple is also called Kutai-ji. On the west bank of the pond stands Amida-do (Amitabha Hall) in which nine buddhist images are enshrined. The whole area of the pond and the garden were cleaned recently to gain a new aspect. The reflection of Amitabha Hall on the pond never ceases to fascinate us with its rich flavor of the Heian Era.
SINAR P NIKKOR 90mm F4.5 f22 1/4 EPR

18 Kinkaku-ji, "A Complete View", Kamakura Era (Kyoto)
It was built by Yoshimasa Ashikaga. The golden pavillion was burnt down in 1950 and reconstructed in 1955. There are more than ten islands of varied sizes in the pond. The golden reflection on the water looks like a mirage of the prosperous old days.
LINHOF KARDAN NIKKOR 90mm F4.5 f22 1/15 EPR

19 Kinkaku-ji, "Taki Stone Grouping", Kamakura Era (Kyoto)
The stone grouping, as well as that of Tenryu-ji, is superbly composed. Rigyo-seki (carp stone), representing a dragon rising to heaven, is found in the central part where water falls. These stones look as if they are about to move at any moment.
LINHOF KARDAN SYMMAR 150mm F5.6 f22 1/2 EPR

20 Sanpo-in, "Sanzon Stone Grouping", Momoyama Era (Kyoto)
The Sanzon stone grouping is derived from the traditional arrangement of three Buddhist images such as the Amitabha triad with an Amitabha at the center and Kannon and Seshi on both sides of it, or the bhaisajyaguru triad. The central stone of this grouping, called the Fujito stone, was delivered to Sanpo-in by Hideyoshi who inherited it from Nobunaga.
LINHOF KARDAN FUJINON 210mm F5.6 f22 1/8 EPR

21 Nijo-jo, "Gogan Stone Grouping", Momoyama Era (Kyoto)
The castle was built by Ieyasu at this site in 1601. For water gardens, stone grouping for shore protection is almost always an important factor of garden making. Stones selected with utmost care and set by skillful hands breathe and reflect light.
LINHOF KARDAN FUJINON 210mm F5.6 f22 1/15 EPR

22 Chijaku-in, "Taki Stone Grouping", Edo Era (Kyoto)
This is the waterfall stone grouping viewed from the northern end of the study room. It somewhat lacks strength when compared to the products of the Kamakura Era but the Edo period surpasses it in elaborateness and delicacy. The form is different from fixed patterns and the expression is free and generous.
LINHOF KARDAN FUJINON 210mm F5.6 f22 1/15 EPR

23 Katsura Rikyu, "Misaki-gata Lantern", Momoyama Era (Kyoto)
There are many shapes of stone lanterns, each of which has its specific name and history. The one in this picture is typical of Misaki-gata lanterns frequently seen in Japanese gardens.
LINHOF KARDAN FUJINON 210mm F5.6 f22 1/15 EPR

24 Shinnyo-in, "Urizane-gata Lantern", Momoyama Era (Kyoto)
The lantern is placed in the Shinnyo-in garden (to be described later). It is made of Muho-to (tomb stone) of the mid-Edo Era with a lamp housing excavated in it. It has an interesting story in that Lord Yoshi-aki of the Ashikaga Shogunate named it.
ZENZA BRONICA ZENZANON 150mm F3.5 f16 1/30 EPR

25 Joju-in, "A Complete View", Edo Era (Kyoto)
The adjacent Kiyomizu-dera is a well-known temple which attracts a great many sightseers. Unbelievable silence reigns in the water garden of Joju-in, set off from the bustle and noises of Kiyomizu. The pond filled with water is beautiful. Here unfold graceful formations integrated with nature as the borrowed landscape.
LINHOF KARDAN SUPERANGULON 75mm F8 f22 1/15 EPR

26 Honpo-ji, "Karetaki Stone Grouping", Momoyama Era (Kyoto)
This is widely known as a product of Koetsu, a versatile artist particularly famous for pottery, gold-lacquering and calligraphy. The special feature of this dry waterfall is a striped stone, set in the lower portion, meant to represent currents of water. Like the dry waterfall portion above, it manifests a splendid creativity.
LINHOF KARDAN SYMMAR 150mm F5.6 f22 1/2 EPR

27 Shinnyo-in, "A Complete View", Momoyama Era (Kyoto)
Here large, scale-shaped stones are used to symbolize a great river, a dynamic technique with magnificent effect. This style of garden-making is a characteristic of the Momoyama Era.
LINHOF KARDAN NIKKOR 90mm F4.5 f22 1/8 EPR

28 Manshu-in, "Ishibashi Stone Grouping", Edo Era (Kyoto)
What attracts visitors to this garden first is this stone bridge. Bridge stones are grouped conspicuously high in the back of the central area and a mountain stream flows under them. The composition inspires a magnanimous mood which testifies to the garden designer's ability.
LINHOF KARDAN FUJINON 210mm F5.6 f22 1/8 EPR

29 Nishi Hongan-ji, "Kame Stone Grouping", Edo Era (Kyoto)
The approximately 760 m² (seven thousand six hundred square feet) wide garden, also known as "the Kokei no Niwa," includes a dry waterfall, two stone bridges, a powerful watershed stone, crane and tortoise stone groupings. Japanese sago palms were planted following the fashion of the time. The carefully constructed landscape can be said to be a masterpiece of Japanese garden design.
LINHOF KARDAN FUJINON 210mm F5.6 f22 1/15 EPR

30 Konchi-in, "Tsuru Stone Grouping", Edo Era (Kyoto)
A worship stone is placed at the center beyond the white sand which spreads, curving gently, in the front. The crane island on the right and the tortoise island on the left are the main features of this garden. They give a sense of grandeur and brightness. The Tsurukubi-ishi (crane neck stone) is particularly majestic.
LINHOF KARDAN NIKKOR 90mm F4.5 f22 1/15 EPR

31 Ikkyu-ji, "Karesansui at the East Garden", Edo Era (Kyoto)
Sojun Ikkyu built his own grave in this temple while he was living. He died here in 1481. The temple has four gardens: the front garden of the graveyard, the south garden, the north garden and the east garden. The east garden, called "the garden of 16 disciples of Buddha," is filled with a spirit worthy of the name of a Zen temple.
LINHOF KARDAN FUJINON 120mm F8 f22 1/8 EPR

32 Reiun-in, "A Complete View", Muromachi Era (Kyoto)
This garden of Reiun-in, a minor temple belonging to Myoshin-ji, has strong characteristic traits. What is signified by the stones arranged in a circle round a boulder as the center in this small garden of only about 60 m² (six hundred square feet). The tremendous volume has a strong appeal to viewers.
LINHOF KARDAN NIKKOR 90mm F4.5 f32 1/2 EPR

33 Nanzen-ji, "A Complete View", Edo Era (Kyoto)
The neighborhood of Nanzen-ji is famous for its scenic beauty, even in Kyoto. The stone grouping surrounded by white sand is set extremely close to the mud wall. The method, also adapted in the garden Daitoku-ji Honbo, is characteristic of the time.
SINAR P NIKKOR 90mm F4.5 f22 1/15 EPR

34 Tokai-an, "A Complete View of the Courtyard", Edo Era (Kyoto)
This garden is the narrowest and smallest of all the gardens shown here. It is a dry landscape with a total dimension of 41.25 m² (four hundred twelve point five square feet). The stones arranged in a straight line are full of variety, while space partitioned by a connecting corridor has a crisp, tense feeling. The garden was made by Toboku Osho in 1814.
SINAR P NIKKOR 90mm F4.5 f22 1/8 EPR

35 Omote Senke, "Around the Zangetsu-tei" Momoyama Era (Kyoto)
Sho-an, Senno Rikyu's son, re-established the Sen family after his father committed harakiri. The garden is adjacent to such tea houses as Fushin-an, Zangetsu-tei and Tensetsu-do. The plants, which are meticulously cared for by hand, create a secluded air and invite visitors to escape a mundane world.
LINHOF KARDAN SUPERANGULON 75mm F8 f22 1/2 EPR

36 Ura Senke, "At the Yuin", Edo Era (Kyoto)
Ura Senke was founded by Genpaku Sotan, a grand-child of Senno Rikyu. There are a number of tea houses, including Konnichi-an, Yuin, Kanun-tei, Mushiki-ken, Totsutotsu-sai, Hosen-sai, and Tairyu-ken in the garden, which are highly valued by educated people as the culmination of wabi, or a taste for the simple and quiet.
LINHOF KARDAN SUPERANGULON 75mm F8 f22 1/2 EPR

37 Mushanokoji Senke, "At the Middle Gate",
Edo Era (Kyoto)
Ichio Soshu, the second son of Sotan, built Kankyu-an at the present Mushanokoji Ogawa Higashi when he retired. This photograph is a portion of the garden's middle gate. The Amigasa gate, with a rustic shingle roof, is suggestive of a tasteful hut. It relaxes us.
LINHOF KARDAN SUPERANGULON 75mm F8 f22 1/2 EPR

38 Yabunouchi Soke, "Around the Machiai",
Edo Era (Kyoto)
Shoichi Tsuruginaka, the founder, served Oda Nobunaga as attendant in charge of tea ceremony. Together with the three Sen families, he contributed much to the development of the art, mainly through the establishment of the Shoin (study room) style tea ceremony. In this Machiai, too, seats for peers are separated from those for ordinary guests.
LINHOF KARDAN SUPERANGULON 75mm F8 f22 1/4 EPR

39 Koho-an, "Sanunjo Tsukubai", Edo Era
(Kyoto)
The Bosen tea room of Koho-an is one of the most prominent of all tea rooms. The Sanunjo shown here is a hermitage-like garden. The water basin is called Fusen-no-Tsukubai. Enshu Kobori created it hoping to develop the art of ceremonial tea-making.
LINHOF KARDAN FUJINON 120mm F8 f16 1/2 EPR

40 Omote Senke, "Fushin-an Tsukubai",
Momoyama Era (Kyoto)
Omote Senke's tea garden is the extreme of simplicity and quietness. The garden forms an unearthly world into which a landscape of deep mountains and gorges appears to have been condensed. This water basin has an air that is suited to the garden. It expresses both practical beauty and beauty of form.
LINHOF KARDAN FUJINON 120mm F8 f22 1 EPR

41 Mushanokoji Senke, "Kankyu-an Tsukubai",
Edo Era (Kyoto)
This type of water basin was made by using the body of a Hokyoin-type (square) stone tower or a multi-story stone tower. Each of the four sides has a buddhist image relief. Known as Shiho-butsu (four-side buddha) no Tsukubai, fine articles of this type are widely used in famous tea houses and tea gardens.
LINHOF KARDAN SYMMAR 150mm F5.6 f22 1/2 EPR

42 Shojuraigo-ji, "A Water Basin", Momoyama
Era (Shiga)
The temple situated at the eastern foot of Mt. Hiei was founded by Eshin Sozu. The top of a stone tower made in the mid-Kamakura Era was placed upside down on a cylindrical shaft for use as a water basin. It has another name, "Nichigetsu no Chozubachi" (water basin of the sun and moon). Its massive voluminousness is beautiful.
LINHOF KARDAN FUJINON 210mm F5.6 f22 1/4 EPR

43 Tokai-an, "Ichimonji Water Basin", Edo Era
(Kyoto)
This was named after its drain hole which is curved in the shape of a short, straight line. Guests wash their mouths and hands while stooping by the Tsukubai as seen in Omote Senke's and the Kankyu-an tea gardens, but these water basins are used for washing while standing. They are also called Ensaki (edge of verandah) Chozubachi.
LINHOF KARDAN FUJINON 210mm F5.6 f22 1/4 EPR

44 Katsura Rikyu, "Katsura-gaki", Momoyama
Era (Kyoto)
Japan has abundant bamboo, which is frequently used for tea houses and Sukiya-style buildings. This bamboo fence is the enclosure erected on the left side of the Katsura Rikyu entrance. The classical design is pleasant. It indicates a boundary between the clergy and the laity.
LINHOF KARDAN SYMMAR 150mm F5.6 f22 1/8 EPR

45 Kinkaku-ji, "Kinkakuji-gaki", Kamakura
Era (Kyoto)
This is a kind of enclosure fence and a variation of Yotsume-gaki (four-eyed fence). For ordinary Yotsume-gaki, horizontal bamboo on the top, as seen in this picture, is not used. The fence is low and the bamboo is spaced widely apart. The plain, rustic style is loved by masters of Cha-no-yu.
LINHOF KARDAN FUJINON 120mm F8 f22 1/8 EPR

46 Koho-an, "Yarai-gaki", Edo Era (Kyoto)
This bamboo fence is erected around the entrance and the stone bridge of Koho-an. It has a manly architectural beauty. The fence, characterized by these ends of strong and sturdy bamboo sharpened like spear heads, has a look of virile, candid refusal.
LINHOF KARDAN SYMMAR 150mm F5.6 f22 1/4 EPR

47 Yabunouchi Soke, "Teppo-gaki", Edo Era
(Kyoto)
Bamboo, with a diameter of a little more than 12 cm (four point eight inch) is split lengthwise and bundled. The bundles, tied with hemp palm rope to inter-twine them, are fixed alternately in the back and front of the horizontal frame. The gentle air of Yabunouchi Soke's tea garden has nothing of the aggressiveness about it that Yarai-gaki has.
LINHOF KARDAN SYMMAR 150mm F5.6 f22 1/8 EPR

48 Mr. Seido's Seibi-en Garden, "Taki Stone
Grouping", Meiji Era (Aomori)
Bugaku Oishi, who had actively engaged in garden-making in Edo, visited Aomori and supervised a number of constructions. Thus, gardens of his style were in fashion in this northern part of Japan. This garden was made by Teiji Obata, one of his disciples. The technique, which was developed in the early Edo period, is found everywhere in ac-curate groupings of stones.
LINHOF KARDAN FUJINON 210mm F5.6 f22 1/8 EPR

49 Motsu-ji, "Nakajima Stone Grouping", Heian Era (Iwate)
Most gardens in the Heian Era were built with large ponds, but only this temple has a pond in which a Shumisen-style stone grouping is laid. When it was erected, it is said that there were three palatial buildings and an arch bridge of about 21m (sixty three feet) long from which to view the Pure Land.
LINHOF KARDAN SYMMAR 150mm F5.6 f22 1/8 EPR

50 Yosan-ji, "Ookarikomi at the Central Part", Momoyama Era (Akita)
Raikyu-ji, Daichi-ji and Jiko-in are a few of the temples famous for their small-leaf box, but this temple's box hedge is large in scale. Big waves and ripples are expressed by it. Although the layout is different, it brings back memories of Raikyu-ji. Gardens using box are rare in the Tohoku district.
LINHOF KARDAN SYMMAR 150mm F5.6 f22 1/8 EPR

51 Gyokusen-ji, "A Complete View", Edo Era (Yamagata)
The principal feature of this garden, made behind the study room, is the pond. A cascade falls from the hillside and three islands are laid in the pond. The trees in the background are thick and in perfect harmony with nature. Stones are laid sharply and forcefully in even detail. The overall view is dynamic and enchanting.
LINHOF KARDAN FUJINON 120mm F8 f22 1/8 EPR

52 Rinno-ji, "The Central Island", Edo Era (Tochigi)
The scale here is great and incorporates Mt. Nantai and the main building of Rinno-ji. The pond stretching from east to west occupies an area of 3,158 m² (thirty-one thousand fifty eight hundred square feet). Azaleas are planted beautifully. The Kanto district has few fine gardens, but this is one of the best of those few.
LINHOF KARDAN NIKKOR 90mm F4.5 f22 1/8 EPR

53 Nonin-ji, "Taki Stone Grouping, Edo Era (Saitama)
This is the only famous garden in Saitama Prefecture. The water garden, which makes use of its hillside location, is meticulously maintained. The waterfall stone grouping on the right hillside is powerful and gorgeous. The cave stone grouping, stone bridge, stone grouping for shore protection and other stone works are fine examples of the art of the time.
LINHOF KARDAN FUJINON 210mm F5.6 f22 1/8 EPR

54 Kencho-ji, "A Complete View", Edo Era (Kanagawa)
The temple was opened by Daikaku Zenji in 1253. As there are lots of cultural assets in the precincts, sightseers keep visiting this temple. Despite the din and bustle, the garden gives a tidy and subdued appearance. Deep vistas are well balanced and express a modest beauty even though the garden has no eye-catching stone grouping.
LINHOF KARDAN NIKKOR 90mm F4.5 f22 1/8 EPR

55 Kyu Shiba Rikyu, "The Central Part of Chitei" Edo Era (Tokyo)
The garden suffered severe war damage but regained its original, beautiful form through the metropolitan government's restoration work after the war. The Chinese-style bridge connecting the island creates an exotic mood. A stone grouping of the Edo Era remains on the hillside of the island.
LINHOF KARDAN NIKKOR 90mm F4.5 f22 1/8 EPR

56 Choraku-ji, "Chitei and Tsukiyama", Edo Era (Shizuoka)
Because nearly 100 dodan azalea trees are planted on a man-made hill at the foot of the mountain, the garden is also called "Dodan no Niwa." The garden, ascribed to Enshu Kobori, is representative of this part of Japan. The view, which incorporates the surrounding nature, is magnificent.
LINHOF KARDAN NIKKOR 90mm F4.5 f22 1/8 EPR

57 Manko-ji, "Sanzon Stone Grouping", Edo Era (Aichi)
The garden is in the backyard of the priests' quarters and is surrounded by thick growths of natural forest. The artificial hill is almost entirely covered with varied stone groupings of a waterfall, Horai-san and Sanzon. It has a sublime appearance which is overwhelming.
LINHOF KARDAN FUJINON 210mm F5.6 f22 1/8 EPR

58 Erin-ji, "Taki Stone Grouping", Kamakura Era (Yamanashi)
This temple is noted for the words: "Clear your mind of all mundane thoughts, and you will find even fire cool." The oldest portion is the Shumisen stone grouping on an upper part of the miniature hill. The other portions were repaired by the orders of Ieyasu, Yoshiyasu and other patrons. With a refined technique employed in all its parts, this can be said to be a deftly constructed garden.
LINHOF KARDAN FUJINON 210mm F5.6 f22 1/8 EPR

59 Daizen-ji, "Tsukiyama Shudan Stone Grouping", Edo Era (Yamanashi)
The Bhaisajyaguru image, to which the temple is dedicated, is a national treasure. It is also called "Budo Yakushi." The establishment of this prominent temple is attributed to Gyoki. On the miniature hill on the left side a Shumisen-style stone grouping and a Tsurushima-style stone grouping co-exist. The method, indicative of manly strength, is well worth our viewing.
LINHOF KARDAN FUJINON 210mm F5.6 f32 1/4 EPR

60 Jizo-ji, "A Complete View", Edo Era (Nagano)
A subtle and profound atmosphere prevails in this garden which was built southeast of the study room behind the main building by making use of limpid spring water. The beauty is doubled by the reflection on the water of the growth of trees above, which were planted following a complex ground plan.
LINHOF KARDAN NIKKOR 90mm F4.5 f22 1/4 EPR

61 Eihou-ji, "Bonnongan Falls", Kamakura Era (Gifu)

Muso Kokushi, a distinguished priest in the Kamakura Era, established this temple. The Kaizan-do building has now been designated a national treasure. On the west side of the pond parted by the Musai bridge the Bonnogan waterfall is located. The sound of the water falling to the bright garden fascinates viewers with its feeling of pureness.
LINHOF KARDAN SYMMAR 150mm F5.6 f22 1/8 EPR

62 Kenroku-en, "Kotoji-gata Lantern", Edo Era (Ishikawa)

Kenroku-en, a famous garden of a feudal lord, was built during the time of Lord Toshinaga, the second chief of the Maeda clan who reigned over the one million-Koku Kaga fief. An attraction of this wide garden is this Kotoji-gata lantern (bridgeshape of a Japanese harp). It is found at the very beginning of the sightseeing course. Tourists swarm there to take snapshots.
LINHOF KARDAN SYMMAR 150mm F5.6 f22 1/8 EPR

63 Rinno-ji, "Multi-story Stone Tower", Edo Era (Tochigi)

This stone tower is placed on the island in the Rinno-ji garden of Nikko. Full-scale multi-story towers are erected for the repose of the dead but those for use in gardens serve to enhance the beauty of the pond rather than for lighting purposes.
LINHOF KARDAN NIKKOR 500mm F8 f22 1/4 EPR

64 Rakuraku-en, "Daikaku-gata Lantern", Era Unspecified (Shiga)

The lantern is used for various practical purposes such as lighting, offerings to a god, repose of the dead and decoration. This one is set on an artificial hill. There is a bridge on its left side and a garden path below it. The lantern serves both for lighting and as a decorative item. Today, it is mostly regarded as a decoration.
LINHOF KARDAN FUJINON 210mm F5.6 f22 1/8 EPR

65 Koraku-en, "Hotaru-gata Lantern", Edo Era (Okayama)

There are only a few thin drum-like lanterns. A hook is provided in the upper portion of the lamp housing to fix the lantern when it is hung. They must have been used frequently since they were installed along the stream flowing toward the Enyo-tei.
MAMIYA R.Z. SEKOR 180mm F4.5 f16 1/15 EPR

66 Kenroku-en, "Seisonkaku Tea Garden", Edo Era (Ishikawa)

This was built as a retreat for Takako, the wife of the 12th Lord Narihiro of the one million-Koku Maeda clan. A winding-water tea garden of this type is rarely seen. Since it is located in snow country, a unique composition with stepping stones laid inside the eaves was used.
LINHOF KARDAN FUJINON 120mm F8 f22 1/2 EPR

67 Seisui-en, "Taki Stone Grouping", Edo Era (Niigata)

This is a stroll style of water garden. The pond has a headland on the east side. Its rugged shore is assumed to have been made following Katsura Rikyu. A Misaki-gata lantern is placed at the end of the headland. The garden belonged to the suburban residences of the Mizoguchi family, the lord of the Shibata fief. The beautiful plants enhance its tastefully restrained appearance.
LINHOF KARDAN SYMMAR 150mm F5.6 f22 1/4 EPR

68 The Site of Mr. Asakura's Residence, "Suwakan Ato Stone Grouping", Momoyama Era (Fukui)

The garden has manly and powerful stone groupings of the Momoyama Era remaining at the sites of Suwa-kan, as shown in this photograph, of Oyudono (the bath house), and of Nanyo-ji. Boulders standing in this garden are meant to represent a waterless cascade and also Horai, the legendary Isle of Eternal Youth. They have an overwhelmingly strong appeal to viewers.
LINHOF KARDAN FUJINON 210mm F5.6 f22 1/2 EPR

69 Kenroku-en, "The Island of Chitei", Edo Era (Ishikawa)

The water garden comprises two parts: the upper Kasumigaike and the lower Hyoike. The original garden was somewhat different from the present one as some work was done on it between the earlier and latter days of the Edo period. The crystal stream flowing out of Mt. Yamazaki runs winding and swirling through the garden.
LINHOF KARDAN FUJINON 210mm F5.6 f22 1/2 EPR

70 Saimyo-ji, "A Complete View", Edo Era (Shiga)

The establishment of Saimyo-ji, one of the three temples on the east side of Lake Biwa, dates back to the Heian Era. The water garden in the backyard of the main building was reduced in scale after damage caused by repeated floods. Nonetheless, the stone groupings of a dry waterfall and the Isle of Eternal Youth on the hillside show us a beauty still intact from the time of their construction.
LINHOF KARDAN NIKKOR 90mm F4.5 f22 1/4 EPR

71 Daichi-ji, "A Complete View", Edo Era (Shiga)

The large-leaf box of Sanbo represents a surge of the sea, and the boat-shaped box on the front left signifies a treasure ship. There is a surprisingly large number of gardens in Shiga Prefecture as is known from the fact that it is called a treasure house of stone arts or fine gardens. This temple with its strong identity is one example.
LINHOF KARDAN SYMMAR 150mm F5.6 f22 1/8 EPR

72 Kitabatake-jinja, "Gogan Stone Grouping", Muromachi Era (Mie)

Originally, this was the garden of the residence of Governor Kitabatake but was later made into a shrine. In this water garden, with its winding stream style, stone groupings are seen from place to place and one keenly senses the spirit of a time which valued simplicity and fortitude. The dry landscape arranged under the sacred tree is particularly full of vigor.
LINHOF KARDAN FUJINON 120mm F8 f22 1/2 EPR

73 Enman-in, "A Complete View", Edo Era (Shiga)
This is one of the temples affiliated with Onjo-ji Mii-dera which is famous for "the evening bell of the Mii Temple." It is believed to have been founded by Enchin. There are two islands representing a crane and a tortoise in the front garden of the main building. The dry waterfall and shore protections are gracefully made to harmonize with cherry blossoms in spring and crimson foliage in autumn, giving the garden an elegant aspect.
LINHOF KARDAN SYMMAR 150mm F5.6 f22 1/8 EPR

74 Fumon-in, "Karetaki Stone Grouping", Edo Era (Wakayama)
There are a number of temples on Mt. Koya which are famous for their founder, Kobo Daishi. Fumon-in is one of them. The garden looks expansive, with the Kameshima, tortoise island, in the north connected by two stone bridges. Many tourists are attracted to this place which is cool in summer. It is hidden in dimness in winter, however, as the snow prohibits anyone from approaching it.
LINHOF KARDAN FUJINON 210mm F5.6 f32 1/2 EPR

75 Negoro-ji, "Taki Stone Grouping", Edo Era (Wakayama)
The garden is in the north part of the study room. The three-step cascade is made on a hillside and a stone to represent a background mountain is set beyond it. The pond is made with two islands, Tsurushima and Kameshima, and two stone bridges. They suggest a refined technique. In addition, a cave and a Yodomari-ishi are formed. The overall landscape is beautiful. The garden is well worth seeing.
LINHOF KARDAN FUJINON 210mm F5.6 f32 1/2 EPR

76 Tentoku-in, "Karetaki Stone Grouping", Momoyama Era (Wakayama)
The temple is the oldest and has the clearest historic record among those within the precincts of Mt. Koya. It was built in 1622 for the salvation of the departed soul of Lady Toshitsune Maeda, the wife of the Lord of Kaga. The garden looks somewhat unkept but the dry waterfall in Sanzon style shown here is most impressive because of the sublime arrangement of stones.
LINHOF KARDAN FUJINON 210mm F5.6 f32 1/2 EPR

77 Hokke-ji, "A Complete View", Edo Era (Nara)
This is a nunnery established by Empress Komyo. The principal image, a wood carving of Juichimen Kannon (Ekadasamukha), which is said to have been modeled after the empress herself, is a masterpiece of the Heian Era. The lovely pond is equipped with a sod bridge and the bed of the stream is covered with small stones. The graceful air is one befitting a nunnery.
LINHOF KARDAN NIKKOR 90mm F4.5 f22 1/8 EPR

78 Gangyo-ji, "A Complete View", Momoyama Era (Nara)
Mt. Yoshino, famous for cherry blossoms, is close to the temple and is thronged with cherry blossom viewers during the season. The waterless portion of the pond is filled with cobblestone and the miniature hill has a Horai stone grouping. The cave stone grouping arranged in a bridge-like form is a focal point of this garden. The limited space is bright and clear and gives a crisp and fresh feeling.
LINHOF KARDAN NIKKOR 90mm F4.5 f22 1/8 EPR

79 Raikyu-ji, "Tsurushima and Ookarikomi", Momoyama Era (Okayama)
Enshu Kobori made this garden sometime around 1604, the year of his appointment as lord of Matsuyama Castle. No other garden follows this one's audacious idea of expressing the surge of the sea by using nothing but small-leaf box. The abstract composition is fascinating. Personally, I prefer flowerless views of this garden to those during the flower season.
LINHOF KARDAN SYMMAR 150mm F5.6 f22 1/8 EPR

80 Koraku-en, "The Central Part of the Chitei", Edo Era (Okayama)
There is an artificial hill called Yuishinzan at the center of the garden. The top of the hill is the best spot for viewing but the angle of this picture, with Okayama Castle seen in the distance, is worth trying. Stone groupings, a winding stream, a zigzag bridge, an arbor, Enyo-tei and other features are scattered nicely. The garden is full of things which are a pleasure to see.
LINHOF KARDAN NIKKOR 90mm F4.5 f22 1/15 EPR

81 Mr. Fukada's Private Garden, "Stone Bridge and Sanzon Stone Grouping", Kamakura Era (Tottori)
The Fukadas are a historic family as is illustrated by the fact that Emperor Godaigo's temporary quarters were made here when he was transferred to Oki Island. It is miraculous that a garden of that time has been privately held and maintained over hundreds of years to this day. The Sanzon stone grouping and the Tsurukame stone grouping are impressive enough.
LINHOF KARDAN NIKKOR 90mm F4.5 f22 1/2 EPR

82 Shukkei-en, "The Island and the Stone Bridge," Momoyama Era (Hiroshima)
This garden was severely damaged by the atomic bomb in August 1945, but was reconstructed to its original state six years later. It was designed by Soko Ueda, a master of ceremonial tea, and the garden winds through various scenic spots including a miniature hill, a sandy beach, a gorge and a waterfall. Its beauty which changes in accordance with the advance of the seasons is most delightful.
LINHOF KARDAN FUJINON 210mm F5.6 f22 1/8 EPR

83 Iko-ji, "Kameshima", Muromachi Era (Shimane)
Sesshu, a great master of painting, made this garden when he was invited by Lord Masuda to come and live in this temple. The shape of the Kameshima, the island, is realistic and easy to recognize. It is filled with energy, as if it were ready to move at any moment. The garden displays its greatest charm when drooping cherry trees on the hillside are in bloom.
LINHOF KARDAN SYMMAR 150mm F5.6 f22 1/8 EPR

84 Mr. Ogawa's Private Garden, "A Complete View", Muromachi Era (Shimane)
The Ogawa family dominated this region in the early Muromachi Era and was respectfully called Wagi Shogun. The shore protection and the dry waterfall at the foot of the hill indicate the skillful construction as well as the finest choice of stone materials. Above all, the dry waterfall in the central part still exists. It is one of the attractions of this garden.
LINHOF KARDAN NIKKOR 90mm F4.5 f22 1/8 EPR

85 Mr. Katsura's Private Garden, "A Complete View", Edo Era (Yamaguchi)
Of numerous stone gardens throughout the country, this is the most peculiar one, and it has a strange effect which is beyond expression. Here, stones are laid over other stones rather than arranged as a group. The technique was used only in this garden, which was given the name of "Tsuki no Katsura."
LINHOF KARDAN NIKKOR 90mm F4.5 f22 1/8 EPR

86 Ritsurin-en, "The Island", Edo Era (Kagawa)
This park with an area of 759,000 m² (seven million five hundred and ninety thousand square feet) is visited by 1.5 million people a year. The forest of Japanese red pines and black pines, the most remarkable feature, is quite impressive. Apart from the care needed to maintain them, their 230 year history here fascinates us.
LINHOF KARDAN FUJINON 210mm F5.6 f22 1/8 EPR

87 Ritsurin-en, "A Complete View", Edo Era (Kagawa)
This photograph was taken from Hirai-ho. Backed by magnificent Shiunzan, the view of Engetsu-kyo, Sei-ko and Kikugetsu-tei is beautiful and stirring. The garden is so spacious that it takes about half a day to go through the six ponds and the 13 artificial hills in it. It can be said to be one of the finest gardens in Japan.
LINHOF KARDAN FUJINON 120mm F8 f22 1/8 EPR

88 Kenroku-en, "Gangyo Stone Bridge", Edo Era (Ishikawa)
The stream flowing through the garden was made by using the abundant spring water available. In the photographed area, the stream, following a winding course, is shallow and transparent. The stone bridge, made of slabs in a tortoise shell shape arranged like a flock of flying wild geese, is unique to this garden and is widely known.
LINHOF KARDAN SYMMAR 150mm F5.6 f22 1/8 EPR

89 Koraku-en, "Yatsuhashi", Edo Era (Okayama)
There are many kinds of Yatsuhashi. They differ in materials such as stone, sod or wood, and are laid using a variety of methods. This one is of a simple construction, with boards arranged alternately, and serves to give variety to the landscape in the foreground.
LINHOF KARDAN SYMMAR 150mm F5.6 f22 1/8 EPR

90 Tamon-ji, "Taki Stone Grouping", Kamakura Era (Tokushima)
Shikoku has many fine gardens, and Tokushima's gardens in particular display wonderful creative skills. This may have some connection to the historic fact that Awa Aoishi (Blue Stone of Awa) has been produced here for a very long time. The mighty, heavy-boned stone grouping looks as if it is about to jump out of the small site.
LINHOF KARDAN FUJINON 210mm F5.6 f22 1/4 EPR

91 Gansho-ji, "A Complete View", Kamakura Era (Tokushima)
Like that of Tamon-ji, this is a small garden. The view around the waterfall stone grouping is almost identical to Ryumon-baku of Tenryu-ji. The beauty is made complete with the view of Enzan-seki and Rigyo-seki, which can be seen in the distance. Once there must have been water here, but it is waterless now and the pond below is dry, too.
LINHOF KARDAN NIKKOR 90mm F4.5 f22 1/4 EPR

92 Hokoku-ji, "A Complete View", Muromachi Era (Ehime)
In this circular water garden, interesting stone groupings are used all along the shore line. The dry waterfall, in bold style in the central part, is typical of the time. This kind of garden is favored by the experts. The careful maintenance which exposes the stones to clear view by intentionally doing away with vegetation is pleasing.
LINHOF KARDAN FUJINON 120mm F8 f22 1/4 EPR

93 Sennyo-ji, "Around the Island", Edo Era (Fukuoka)
Formally called Raisan Sennyo-ji Daihi Ouin, this is a great temple that had 300 houses of monks at one time. The garden in front of the study room, surrounded by secluded forest, is particularly beautiful in autumn when the leaves turn color. The stone grouping looks unattended but the quiet air around the two islands makes viewers feel very peaceful.
LINHOF KARDAN NIKKOR 90mm F4.5 f22 1/2 EPR

94 Mr. Mori's Private Garden, "Taki Stone Grouping", Edo Era (Kagoshima)
Chiran-cho, where Mr. Mori's garden is situated, was a commando base of the former Imperial Navy. In this area, residences of higher-ranked Samurai stand side by side, each with a garden of dry landscape which is thronged with sightseers. Among them, only Mr. Mori's garden is a water garden. The stone grouping reminds us of the gardens of Okinawa.
LINHOF KARDAN FUJINON 210mm F5.6 f22 1/4 EPR

95 Suizen-ji, "A Complete View", Edo Era (Kumamoto)
The area is rich with spring water. The miniature hill molded after Mt. Fuji mirrored on the crystal clear water gives a strong impression to visitors. Tadatoshi Hosokawa began constructing the garden in 1637. There are three islands in the south and north which are connected through dales.
LINHOF KARDAN NIKKOR 90mm F4.5 f22 1/8 EPR

96 Mr. Ishigaki's Private Garden, "A Complete View", Edo Era (Okinawa)
Although the main island of Okinawa was totally devastated during the war, Ishigaki Island narrowly escaped such damage. The existing garden is of value as a reference when considering the lost gardens of the main island. It was made by Unjo Machika, a gardener from Shuri. Kaishoku-seki, used in the stone grouping on the artificial hill and in other places, gives it an integrated look and express the feeling of a southern country full of brightness.
LINHOF KARDAN NIKKOR 90mm F4.5 f22 1/8 EPR

AFTERWORD

Initially aspiring to be a news photographer, I have taken pictures of gardens for over approximately 30 years. It all began when I was introduced to Master Mirei Shigemori (a landscape researcher) by his son, Mr. Koen Shigemori, a photograph critic today.

The first garden was the Sandai Komyozenin Garden at the Tofuku-ji Temple in Kyoto. When I showed Master Shigemori some feasibly acceptable photographs I had taken after commuting to the garden for 3 days, he said, "They're black pictures, aren't they?" (Pictures at that period were monochrome.) The pictures had strong subjective characteristics where the dark areas were blurred and the highlighted areas appeared to jump out. It took me awhile to comprehend what he meant by them being black pictures. The leading stone groupings such as the Taki, Sanzon, and Enzan group of stones were frequently located in dark sites shaded by large bushes and shrubs. At that time I had no reason to know which was the Sanzon or the Taki. As the white sand shone brilliantly in the sunlight, the gigantic rocks appeared black and crouching. Absorbed in the sight before me I became engrossed with snapping the shutter. They had become black pictures. Only the sparkling white sand and black masses of rocks were pictured.

As time went by I made a pledge to myself. I had to somehow capture the stone groupings, the plots of ground, the stepping stones, and other details in my pictures. I came to understand that as long as I remained ignorant of the elements and materials that composed a garden, I could never truly call them pictures of gardens. You could say I was intent on depicting the bare ground, in particular.

Whatever the intentions of the photographer, whether he may take pictures of the entrance to the tearoom, stone wash basins, central gate, stepping stone, yakuishi, stone lanterns, etc., there is significance and meaning in them. Photographers have almost given up on photographing places like the interior of tea ceremony rooms which are under study. Unaware of these things, it is not surprising that my photos appeared primarily black; they were not photographs of gardens. From this experience I began striving to photograph Master Shigemori's works in hopes of receiving his praise. Learning to distinguish good gardens from bad ones, I started to understand what a garden was. However, this itself was insufficient and I retook one picture after another. Master Shigemori who was lenient in the beginning became stricter with each passing year, giving out directives on the pictures which involved moving from narrow localized areas to broader views and vice versa. Focusing on narrow localized areas, I was taught every detail concerning the essence of stone grouping. Reflecting back, this is one way of teaching that distinguished the period. Because Master Shigemori also took photographs himself, I could understand his teachings. I am indebted to him.

I have heard this from photographers specializing in flowers. When portraying a flower one must know the name of the flower and the species as well as the origin, in addition to knowing the number of stamens, the shape of pistils, the number of petals, and more circumstantially the shape of the leaves in order to produce a good picture incorporating all these elements. When I heard this, I thought how it resembled taking pictures of gardens.

At this time I had an offer to do a photo collection from Mr. Kakuzo Akahira of Graphic-sha Publishing Co., Ltd. The theme was to be on gardens through the seasons, however, I could not select among the various seasons anything to satisfy me. I was at loss as the pictures taken were not natural scenic ones. Again, I ran into the problem as to whether the gardens could be used in a photo collection or a collection of various works.

In the case of gardens, they are themselves works of art. Landscape designers who are devoted to the art of gardening exist today and continue to transmit the beauty that has taken hundreds of years to perfect.

Facing my camera towards the subjects I press the shutter. Aren't they ultimately just mere reproductions? The photographs of gardens by predecessors, the statue of Buddha, the buildings... aren't they all reproductions? However, there is no mistake from the angle and position I have selected they belong to me. This is fine. This is how it is done. These photographs are the results of this selection.

Master Mirei who taught me everything is no longer with us now, however, I hope you will be able to see his teachings demonstrated in my work and I look forward to your comments. In conclusion, I would like to extend my warmest gratitude to Mr. Shimpei Kusano who contributed the preface and Mr. Shigemori and designer Hiroto Kumagai for their advice. In addition, I would like to thank Mr. Akahira of Graphic-sha Publishing Co., Ltd., who was in charge of the planning and progress and especially to the former Master Mirei who I wish could have seen it. God bless you.

Haruzo Ohashi